Denise KENYON-ROUVINEZ
GABS

Who, Me?

FAMILY BUSINESS SUCCESSION
A PRACTICAL GUIDE FOR THE NEXT GENERATION

Lombard Odier Darier Hentsch & Cie
Banquiers privés depuis 1796

FAMILY ENTERPRISE PUBLISHERS
Division of The Family Business Consulting Group, Inc.®

Family Enterprise Publishers®
1220-B Kennestone Circle
Marietta, Georgia 30066 U.S.A.
800-551-0633
www.efamilybusiness.com

Copyright ©2007 Family Enterprise Publishers®
ISBN: 1-891652-19-2

Contents

Foreword, Thierry Lombard	7
Introduction	13
I. Succession	15
II. Communication	33
III. The family	47
IV. The name	57
V. Identity	65
VI. Preparing to join the business	73
VII. Working in the company	87
VIII. The shareholders	101
IX. Challenges	109
Conclusion	123
Bibliography	125
Detailed table of contents	126
Index	128

"Somehow the business invited itself to every meal."

FOREWORD

To the next generations

What is it about family businesses that makes them such an object of fascination? Without a doubt, the way they blur the line between factory and home, between work and family, between colleague and cousin, between parent and peer. Their corporate culture, shaped by ancestral tradition, inherited contradiction, unwritten laws, filial piety, stifled rebellion, and lifelong devotion to a trade. Their *family spirit*, shared, across borders, by children raised from their earliest days to take on a particular profession because that was the wish of their father, their mother, their grandparents, uncles, siblings, and the firm.

These are the sources of a family business's strength. Since man started trading, the passing on of family businesses to the next generation has given the world a large number of success stories. To this day, the family business continues to play a uniquely important economic role. But at the personal level, taking over a family firm brings difficulties that can only really be understood by those directly involved. What an unbelievable opportunity, to "automatically" be the next in line. But at the same time, what a responsibility, what a burden, what pressure, and what constraints

Who, Me?

This book is intended first and foremost for those who, like me, found themselves at the age of twenty leading the "next" generation of a family business, beset by all the doubts that such a position brings. The seasoned family business expert Denise Kenyon-Rouvinez has provided us with a host of observations, as well as her most tried-and-tested remedies to help today's next generations face up to a series of difficult choices. And to present some of the situations that await those generations in a more humorous light, we have called upon another specialist, the inimitable Gabs.

For 20 years, Gabs has been capturing our everyday life in pen and ink, our ceaseless back-and-forth between life at the office and life at home, between the intimate and the work-related. He seems to share our belief that the line separating these two aspects of our existence is exquisitely fine. What is certain is that he misses none of the subtle interplay of business and family, nor the travails of those whose destiny was handed to them in the cradle. He holds up a mirror in which we may see ourselves and laugh, and thus indulge in what Jules Renard calls the healthiest form of lucidity.

We offer this user's guide for successors as our way of contributing to the dialogue between the generations. We hope it will convince those at the starting line that the goal is worth the effort. For while a family business is undeniably a long-term undertaking, it is also—first and

FOREWORD

foremost—a magnificent adventure, an ambitious project shared with one's nearest and dearest, and a management mind-set that ranks quality, responsibility, ethics, and long-range vision among its priorities. And if the family business is to remain a model, the very best must work together, in each generation.

Our experience has convinced us that the challenge is worth taking up—indeed, that it can be a reward in its own right. As a firm of private bankers since 1796, we are devoutly attached to our calling, and there is no mystery here. It is our clients' continuing happiness that keeps us walking in the footsteps of our ancestors, applying the same rules of the trade for seven generations. Understanding the complex mix of a personality, assets, a family, and a business to obtain the very best result: this is our calling, our family tradition, and our professional creed—our vision of a sustainable enterprise, no matter what generation happens to be in charge.

Thierry Lombard

To Olivia
To Marguerite

*And to the next generation of our family businesses,
who hold a part of our future in their hands.*

Acknowledgments

We would like to express our particular thanks to the people who contributed to this book :

Alexandre ARNBÄCK and Thierry LOMBARD (Lombard Odier Darier Hentsch & Cie)
Christine BLONDEL (INSEAD)
Lucie and Nicole FAVRE (Monodor)
Suzanne HANSON and Joachim SCHWASS (IMD : International Institute for Management Development)
Alexis LOMBARD
Olivier de RICHOUFFTZ (FBN : The Family Business Network)

We are also deeply grateful to the many families and to the many young people who, over the years, have shared with us their experiences, their difficulties, and their enthusiasm for family business.

INTRODUCTION

In this book we discuss succession, primarily from the point of view of the next generation. We also look at family relations, conflict resolution, and entering the family business. The book's focus-and its originality-is its exploration of identity, of the various roles within a family business, and of the challenges facing the next generation.

In writing it we have come in contact with parents, successors, and academics, all of whom have spoken openly about failures and successes. They have recalled frustrations, fears, and doubts; but they have also spoken of pride, the joys of sharing, and of happiness.

When we talk about successors within the context of this book, we mean both women and men. Both face similar situations, doubts, and challenges. Our aim is to help young people understand that many other successors share their concerns, and that there are tools and resources available to help.

I
Succession

Any discussion of the next generation naturally begins with the issue of succession. When does succession begin? How long does it last? These are just two of the questions raised when families talk about their businesses. In fact, planning for a succession begins in the cradle, continues during the child's upbringing and the sharing of family values. Most experts agree, however, that an active succession period should last between five and ten years if it is to provide the best conditions for both the family and the business.

Although "succession" is typically understood to refer to the taking over of the management of a family business, the key to the process is actually the transfer of corporate ownership (shares and voting rights), since ownership succession is what actually confers decision-making power.

Succession is a period of profound change, and hence a time of great strain, for both the business and the family. It is often very emotional and fraught with uncertainty.

A joint venture between two generations

Something we have heard many, many times from young and talented people is: "We find it difficult to plan our career, because no one has actually said that there is a place for us in the family business. We would like to play a part, but we aren't exactly counting on it. We're waiting for some sort of signal."

This wait-and-see attitude is typical in family businesses: it stems from young people's fear of offending their elders. At the same time, those in charge take this reticence as a troubling indication of the next generation's lack of interest or ambition, when in fact just the opposite may be true.

It is therefore important to emphasize that a successful transition is far from simply a passing of the baton from one generation to the next, with the senior generation directing the process and laying down the rules. Instead, it is generally the product of a true partnership between generations, with both playing important roles and expressing their opinions.

Sharing out

Unless the chosen successor is an only child, the division of things is always part of a succession process. Duties, power, funds, ownership of properties—all have to be distributed. Parents usually want to treat their children fairly. However, it can be difficult to distribute things equally among multiple successors. For example, there is usually only one CEO position, and many family firms are too small to allow for more than one successor to take over the management of the business. And, if there is any family real estate to be bequeathed, it typically consists of just one home.

Unless it is extremely well planned, an unequal division can lead to conflict. Children do, albeit for the most part unconsciously, measure their parents' love partly in terms of what they receive from them. When a family business is divided unequally, those who feel they have drawn the short straw may go through long periods of doubt and incomprehension, which can in turn develop into resentment of their "luckier" siblings.

A well-planned division, especially when the reasons behind it are clearly communicated, can help the next generation to feel at ease with the decisions made, even if the split is unequal.

A fair process

What really matters is not so much whether the division is equitable or if the next CEO is the right choice, but rather the way in which these issues are perceived by the successors. Even the most painstakingly equal division may be seen as outrageously unjust, for example where two brothers are each given 50% of a business in which only one of them works. That brother may find it unfair that his share is not larger, since he carries the responsibility for the firm and its risks. By the same token, many unequal divisions may be perceived as perfectly reasonable.

The crucial factor influencing perceptions of fairness is the way the division has been performed and presented—the process. A fair process requires good communication and the involvement of everyone at the earliest possible stage. The children's participation should depend on their age and the issues under discussion. Ample opportunity should be given for people to express their opinions freely. There should also be clear rules for both the company and the succession, and these must be applied even-handedly to all concerned.[1]

---

1. L. van der Heyden, C. Blondel, R. S. Carlock, 2005.

The family constitution

The family constitution, also known in Europe as the family protocol, is a document setting out rules governing the relationship between the family and the business. It covers such matters as who may work in the business, what skills are required for its senior management, who may become a shareholder, and who may sit on the board. It is a practical way to achieve clarity and transparency, and, as such, can promote trust and drive performance.

Since no two family businesses are the same, there is no standard template for a family constitution. It is vital for the family constitution to be drafted fairly, and applied equitably. The more family members participate in drafting the document, the more willing they will be to view the concepts as their own, and the more willing they will be to respect its values. Such rules must be communicated and applied to all family members. The family constitution will let the next generation know what is expected of them in terms of education, training, and skills, both human and technical. Thus equipped, the next generation can devote themselves fully to the task of living up to those standards.

The role of the parents

Parents play multiple roles in the succession process. First and foremost, they must make the business (and its products) attractive, teach their children the value of a job well done, and train, motivate, and nurture the next generation. When the time comes, they must also find the courage to retire and leave the business in their children's hands. This is by no means an easy task, and there are numerous successors still waiting to take over the reins at the ripe age of 50 or 60. Founders generally have the hardest time during the transition: feeling after all, that this business is like their child, and they are abandoning it. This feeling is also coupled with the fear of no longer being useful.

A recent IMD[1] study shows that, in the most successful family businesses, parents tend initially to be protective: they are very close to their children, directing their studies and passing on their beliefs and values. At a later stage, however, they let go and give the next generation a large measure of freedom.[2]

---

1. IMD : *International Institute for Managment Development.*
2. J. Schwass, 2005

The role of the children

For its part, the next generation must begin by expressing its motivation (or lack of it) to pursue the business and tend to its products. This motivation need not be an ambition to run the company, but it should include the desire to play a role there, whether as an employee or on the board of directors, or as a shareholder. Next there must come a commitment to the family's values, a willingness to undergo training and to prove oneself. In this way successors will earn respect, both from the company's employees and from the family itself.

The next generation can also facilitate and accelerate the succession process by understanding the reasons for the previous generation's reluctance to let go. In particular, they must demonstrate their sense of duty and commitment to the business, its employees, and its products. They should ensure that the elder generation is financially secure, with guaranteed income and a decent retirement. The greater this financial security, the easier it will be for the previous generation to hand over the business and its shares in it.

A success story

Here's an exemplary success story. Four brothers were allowed to choose their own roles in the family business based on their talents and true ambitions. Not only were their parents ready to leave, they also encouraged the dialogue between the children, and let them choose the management model they wished to put in place for their generation. In the end, each son took the position in which he felt at ease and where he could prosper. The current managing director is in fact not the eldest son, but rather the brother with the greatest leadership abilities and the best skills for this particular job. He was unanimously chosen for the task by his brothers, and he has been able to win the respect of his parents and employees.

II

Communication

A family business succeeds and fails by its communication. Inadequate, poor, or non-existent communication leads directly to conflict. Good communication requires an ability to talk as well as listen. This is all the more crucial during succession, when everyone is already on edge.

Communication within the family

Family members—parents and children, siblings, cousins—do not always find it easy to communicate when they are caught up in their work and under pressure. This is precisely when the communication of important things like family values, and words of love and encouragement, can be neglected.

One communication style to be avoided at all costs is inconsistency and ambiguity. Someone who counsels "Do whatever you like, it doesn't matter whether you join the business or not," must truly mean it. Otherwise they risk feeling disappointed and angry with children who actually follow their advice.

Communication within the business

Employees, too, will have their share of doubts and fears during the succession period. "Will the family go on investing in the business? Will they keep my position? Will the business relocate? Will the next generation take my job away?" A clear announcement of the arrival of family members in the company and what the family's intentions are for the business will help calm such fears. Failing to provide such crucial information means giving free rein to rumors and conspiracy theories. When employees understand the family's motives, they are more motivated, have more energy and devote themselves to the company's success.

Communication outside the business

All important changes in the decision-making chain, including the retirement of one generation and the arrival of another, must also be communicated to clients, suppliers, banks, and other stakeholders.

Expectations

Many young people have misconceptions of what is expected of them. "My uncle has no children," they say to themselves, "so he'll be counting on me to take over"; while the uncle may have completely different plans. Or they think, "My brother's already in the company, so there's no place for me," while in fact the family is waiting for him to join the business to start up a new unit.

Parents are not immune either. "I don't think my son is really up to working in the company," thinks a father, "but I don't dare tell him, it would shatter his illusions." That son, meanwhile, might well be thinking, "If only I could go and do something else! I'm so bored here and I don't really like our products. I'm only staying on to please my dad."

It is crucial to talk to one another in order to clarify the positions and the expectations of all concerned, and thus prevent and minimize any conflicts.

Conflict

Conflicts are an inherent feature of family businesses. Those experiencing them should remember that their family or company is probably no different from any other.

Conflict is a normal fact of life. It arises chiefly because two people rarely view a situation from the same perspective. For example, shareholders who work in a family business may well feel that only those who play an active part deserve to be rewarded. Shareholders who do not work in the business, on the other hand, will argue they have every right to their dividends. If they feel excluded from decisions, they may press for dividends even if it means jeopardizing the company's investment policy. Giving non-employed shareholders a role in the decision-making process, or in the family council, will narrow the gap between them and the "actives." If their involvement is genuine, and the motive sincere, the pressure to distribute dividends should be reduced.

Conflict that gives each party the opportunity to voice their concerns is healthy. Both sides often have legitimate concerns. Taking both into account can actually help to fine-tune strategy and improve decisions.

Managing conflicts

All the same, accepting conflict as natural and healthy doesn't make it easier to deal with. It can also be very emotionally charged, distracting those who should be devoting their time and energy to managing the company.

If the discord becomes serious, a family business consultant should be called in. Before matters reach this point, however, the family can use some basic precepts to help prevent conflict, and manage it when it occurs:

– *Set down clear rules* for succession and for joining the company, and in general for all forms of family/business interaction. This avoids raising false expectations.
– *Help* those who will not be inheriting or working in the business find a role for themselves in another sphere; otherwise they will probably feel discouraged and left out. Family harmony will surely benefit.
– *See the adult and not the child* in professional relationships, and treat children working at the company with respect.

- *Keep an open mind* and avoid wounding remarks such as, "That will never work" or "If you put him in charge of the unit he'll ruin us."
- *Support the in-laws*, especially when a prenuptial agreement is required. Help them understand why such an agreement is necessary, and assure them that it doesn't mean they are being excluded from the family.
- *Allow disagreement to be voiced* and be prepared to hear the reasons for it. This may help the family to see things in a new light and to grow stronger.
- *Adopt an inclusive attitude*: Say "Let's deal with this together." Talk, listen carefully, establish social connections, hold family events: all these things help foster contact and put differences aside for a while.
- *Seek harmony – and allow it to emerge*: The way the family functions will be a significant factor in determining whether the transition is a failure or a success.

III
The family

Numerous studies have shown that successful family businesses are significantly more profitable over the long term than other businesses. A strong, unified, harmonious family is thus one of the best assets a company can have. But family also means feelings—passions, jealousies, and feuds that are not always easy to manage during the day-to-day life of a business.

And, while parent-child relations as well as those between cousins can be challenging, the most difficult relationship in a business context is that between brothers and sisters. Siblings need to be particularly careful about maintaining a balance in their relations, whether or not they all work in the family business. Parents and spouses play a key role in helping them keep the lines of communication open. Unless all do their utmost to keep their relationship healthy, siblings' resulting power struggles can run out of control, with disastrous results.

The definition of "family"

The word "family" typically conjures up images of parents, grandparents, siblings, cousins—in short, blood relations. In reality, though, it also includes spouses (the in-laws), and—with the increasing prevalence of reconstituted families—half-brothers and half-sisters or stepsiblings. The more the family grows, the greater the importance of guidelines governing who can work in the business or become a shareholder, and who cannot. Without such clear rules, feelings of injustice and frustration are bound to arise, and will inevitably poison family relations.

Some families prohibit spouses from holding shares in the business, while others welcome them; some divide shares equally, and some actually keep spouses as shareholders even after a divorce, so as to maintain cordial relations with the children from the marriage. Whatever the model chosen, it is crucial that its impact on the next generation be understood. A daughter may find it unjust that she is a shareholder while her half-brother is barred from holding any of the company's stock.

"I LOVE PLAYING HAPPY RECONSTITUTED FAMILY: I'D LIKE THE DIVORCED HALF-SISTER!"

The tools available to families

A sustainable family company is built on two equally crucial foundations: a healthy business and a healthy family. Successful business families are careful to devote the same amount of energy to each. Before long, young people are liable to find the familial part of the arrangement restricting and oppressive. A little organization and a few rules, however, are all that it takes for things to remain pleasant and for alliances of love and trust to be forged among its members.

Family spirit

Successful families often begin by making a clear statement of their common ideals and beliefs—their identity. They share strong values that have lasted through several generations and can be found in the corporate culture. They know their history and are proud of their origins. And they love to tell family anecdotes, often funny stories, like the one about crusty old Uncle Henry, who never suffered fools gladly, or moving ones, about a grandfather who supported a deceased employee's widow and children.

A code of conduct

This is a very simple document outlining how family members organize their relations. It points out such things as the need to avoid conflict in front of staff or clients, or during social occasions, out of respect for one another. It also sets out how decisions should be made and issues resolved.

Family meetings

Family meetings are occasional, formal events. While providing an opportunity for the family to relax and enjoy itself, they principally serve to regulate relations between the family and its business. In particular, they are a forum for reinforcing and transmitting values, a way for the family to keep abreast of developments in the firm, and an opportunity for each individual member to identify with the business. Above all, however, they should be an occasion for the family to talk about the business, leaving them free to focus on the family the rest of the time.

The family council

When a family grows in size, it may be useful to create a family council comprising a few elected members whose principal task is to develop rules (a family constitution) and to prepare for succession.

IV

The name

A majority of family businesses are eponymous; in other words, the company bears the name of the family that founded it. Well-known examples include Ford, S.C. Johnson, Michelin, Peugeot, Sainsbury, Koc, Kanoo, Heineken, and Benetton.

The impact of the name on the next generation

This dual nature of the name (family and company) means that it acts in two conflicting ways: as a motivating factor and a limitation. Many young people say that, although proud of their name, they feel it puts them constantly on the defensive. It forces them to watch how they behave and avoid drawing attention to themselves, since they feel responsible for the image they project of the company and the family. It is as if they can never completely "let go". In others it engenders an arrogance that prompts them to exploit their position for personal advantage. Yet others make the most of the situation by adopting a philosophical and detached approach; they seek first and foremost to be themselves and establish a distinct identity within the boundaries of the family name.

Striking the right balance

The name of the business itself may act as a unifying factor, creating motivation and promoting family harmony. For this reason, families should pay close attention to its name. Inevitably, however, the dual identity focuses attention on the family and puts pressure on parents. They must decide how far they should allow their children to develop and make the mistakes that are an inevitable part of growing up, without damaging the reputation of the family or compromising their future career within the business.

Parents can probably best help their offspring by setting a good example (actions, after all, speak louder than words), and by making them proud of their name. This pride will generally spring from an understanding of the family's history and that of the family firm; from the amusing or embarrassing anecdotes that are told; and from a love of the products and of a job well done. Pride in the family name will in turn make it easier to strike a balance between the sense of duty, and the carefree spirit which is—or ought to be—the prerogative of youth.

A powerful management tool

If a company is well known, the name of the family will be too; and the better known the company, the higher the profile of its products and services. This may, as has already been noted, be either a positive or a limiting factor for the family. But it should be remembered that the name can also be an exceptionally powerful communication and marketing tool for the company and its products.

Customers and consumers like to recognize themselves in products. The fact that those products are linked to families makes it easier to identify with them: "If that recipe was invented by his grandmother, it could just as easily have been my grandmother who came up with it. What's more, it's bound to be delicious, because it will have been created with love by someone determined to give the best to her children and grandchildren."

The presence of the family behind the product also gives a feeling of security—"If they were around eighty years ago, they will still be around tomorrow, so I can buy their products with absolute confidence"—and is seen as a guarantee of quality.

V
Identity

How can one stay true to oneself while respecting the family's values and its model? How can one be a good employee while remaining true to one's own ambitions? Faced with the constraints imposed by the business and the family itself, many young people find it difficult to establish their own identity. When are they themselves? When are they what the family or firm expects of them?

"Can I really do things my own way? If my way is wrong, won't I be the generation everyone talks about: the one that failed? I can just see the four or five generations that came before me, each seeming to be brimming with talent, looking down on me." As if life wasn't already stressful enough…

One young man was the appointed heir to a very large family business which his mother ran with such skill that it grew tenfold under her control. He told us he wanted to set up and manage his own company before taking over the family business, to prove to himself that he was capable of doing it. He wanted to be able to look straight in the eye of those who couldn't wait for him to mess up.

The need to exist

What many young people want most is the opportunity to be themselves and live their personal and professional lives in accordance with their own choices. But they are unsure whether this is possible in the context of a family business. They need to be shown that it is possible.

Many speak of a sense of loneliness—they feel misunderstood not only by their families, but also by their friends. They face choices such as "Why don't you come on vacation with us this summer instead of doing another internship in the company?" Ultimately, they find themselves torn between opposing worlds, unable to decide which they belong to—the world of education or the world of business, their friends or their family, the past or the future.

The main priority is to help them find their own place and play their own distinctive role, whether or not they choose to work in the family company. After all, management is not the be-all-and-end-all: there are plenty of other roles to fill in a family business. Everyone can contribute to the company's development, even if they opt for a career elsewhere.

The fundamental questions

Identifying the job or the career one wants is the first step towards feeling free to choose, motivated, and able to assert one's own personality. Some questions need to be answered with absolute honesty:

— Do I want to work in the family business?
— Have I decided that for myself, or is it what my parents want?
— Am I choosing this because it would give me a guaranteed income?
— If I go into the business, what role would I like? What kind of work motivates me?
— Am I more likely to realize my potential inside the company or outside?
— If I decide not to work in the business, what should I go into? Something similar, or something different?

Successors who work in the family business despite having no desire to do so will help neither themselves nor the company. Ultimately, they will run the risk of being bad at what they do—or adequate at best—simply because they will not like their job, and know that they could develop more fully somewhere else. Being honest with oneself is the first step towards building one's own identity.

VI
Preparing to join the business

Some say that preparation should begin at the cradle. There is a great deal of truth to this: family values, after all, are instilled from birth. So too are the passion for a product, pride in belonging to the family, and the love of a job well done.

Many families encourage their children to join in the company's activities from a very early age, sometimes even before the age of ten. They do this not by making them work long hours, but by giving them small jobs at the weekend or taking them to informal meetings with clients or staff. Such encounters with the grown-up world often develop a child's pride and pleasure in accomplishing something useful. While it must remain fun and relaxed, this phase of training is important because it socializes while giving the child a taste of work life. And, in trades which require taste, dexterity, and mastery (such as confectioner, saddler, goldsmith, winemaker or watchmaker), it can help them to rapidly feel at ease with the most delicate aspects of production when they start to learn the trade.

Studies and training

Families often lay down precise rules about the training and studies necessary for a family member intending to join the business. Requirements can vary considerably—a summer internship at the company, a specialized apprenticeship (to learn the trade), a university degree, an MBA or foreign language skills. Increasingly, too, families are expecting the next generation to spend between two and five years learning the ropes at another company.

In fact, working outside the family business can often provide a much-needed breath of fresh air. It can be a period of freedom that provides an opportunity to take one's own decisions and risks. It also offers the next generation a taste of doing without the privileges that they may have come to expect. As one young man talking about his first experience outside the family business explained: "This lady took me on out of pity, because she could see how terrible I was during the interview. She was tough, but she taught me everything I know. She gave me a real chance."

The benefits of training

While successors may find these training phases overly long, they are a worthwhile experience. The goal is not simply for the next generation to accumulate as many degrees as possible or become overqualified, but to learn something of real benefit to them.

The first task facing young people will be to establish themselves as credible employees within the firm. Good references and relevant qualifications will give them confidence in themselves as well as providing them with an idea of their value on the market.

At the same time, no business has a guaranteed future, and proper training can help provide a safety net, a way of finding a new job or starting up one's own company if need be. Otherwise there is the risk of winding up like one young man whose success within the family business was of no use to him when it folded. His lack of outside references made it impossible for him to find work. His application was routinely dismissed as coming from a "daddy's boy," someone who had made it only because of his name. In the end he had no choice but to set up his own business.

The role of the family

The family plays multiple roles. Among the firsts are to prepare the children, and to understand their various talents and thus to help foster their skills.

The family will need patience and to be prepared to accept that people in their early to mid-twenties have the right to find themselves. Young adults may well also go through a phase of not knowing what they want to do with their lives. Organized internships with the company can increase familiarity with the business, and give potential successors a taste for it.

However, the family's main task is twofold. First, it must enforce its own rules on training. If a particular function calls for an MBA, the family must see to it that this criterion is met. Otherwise it may be seen to favor those who do not follow the rules while frustrating those who do. Second, the family must ensure that its rules are not too demanding, bearing in mind the size and nature of its business. Many young heirs accumulate numerous qualifications, and in so doing develop ambitions that can no longer be satisfied by the family company.

Should I or shouldn't I?

The period immediately before entering the family business is often the hardest on young people. It is a time of hesitation and doubt. Chief among the worries are:

1. *Fear of not being up to the task.* This concern comes partly from the weight of past generations, and partly from a fear that one is not the equal of those presently in control. But it is also an error—these are, after all, young people of 20, 25, or 30 comparing themselves with a generation at the peak of its career. For its part, the senior generation should talk about the doubts they had when they were young, and speak about the failures and difficulties they experienced. This will give the next generation the confidence to know they have the right to make mistakes, and more importantly, time to mature.
2. *There is nothing left to be accomplished.* After three or four generations, a family business may give the impression of coasting along quite nicely. Naturally, nothing is set in stone, and there is always room for improvement. Still, doubts may arise, especially when the next generation sees classmates embarking on apparently fabulous careers with multinationals, featuring generous salaries and exotic locations.

3. *The connection—or lack of connection—with the product.* This may be expressed as an absence of interest, and here the response should be to foster enthusiasm for a particular skill rather than a product. Alternatively, it may involve a sense of shame about Dad's business, especially if it is one regarded as dirty (e.g. the cleaning or decontamination industry). Another example involves the third generation of sons in one delicatessen dynasty that specialized in sausage and salami. After going to university, they could no longer see themselves working in that kind of sector, and sold the company. Perhaps by looking beyond the product and attempting to create a successful brand, other people in their position might have liked to go into the exporting business and thus develop their own pleasure in the family's traditional activity.
4. *Signing away one's career.* The decision to enter the family business sometimes brings with it the anxious feeling of signing away one's working life. It is as if they are losing their freedom, and have reached the point of no return.

Appreciating the reasons for a young person's hesitancy about entering the family business should be the starting point for a dialogue. Once understanding has been reached, proposals and compromises can be developed that will alleviate their fears and help them make the leap.

VII

Working in the company

"I had no choice, I had to take over the business. I didn't want to force my children into it, but today I see things a bit differently. Ultimately you need to work in a company and understand it in order to love it." As this company's CEO rightly says, you have to experience a firm at first hand to appreciate it and comprehend the full extent of the passion that can develop around a product and a success.

It won't always be easy, but the fact is that family businesses frequently offer unparalleled career opportunities and give young people a chance to work on exciting projects. Nevertheless, new recruits will still have to demonstrate a high level of professionalism and prove that they are deserving of trust.

Older members of the family will have to treat them as responsible employees—to view them as adults and no longer as children. They have grown up, after all. Old and young alike must work together to ensure a smooth transition, keeping employee motivation high and ensuring that the best employees remain with the company.

Relationships with employees

Among the first things a successor needs to do are to establish a relationship with employees, to demonstrate his or her credibility, and to become a true leader. These things need to be done continuously throughout his or her career with the firm. It is a challenging task to avoid the perception that one is there solely because Dad owns the company. Earning respect as a leader of the family business is difficult when one is still remembered as the child who used to steal apples from the local orchard.

It will be necessary to look people in the eye and confront any jealousy and spite, while retaining a clear understanding of what motivates employees in their relationship with the family. Some are petty-minded, some self-serving; others will be utterly loyal. It is not always easy to distinguish the good from the bad, but over the years judgment improves and it becomes easier to identify who is sincere and who is not.

Above all, it will also be essential to reach a working arrangement enabling cooperation between employees who are also family members. This can be tricky, as differences of opinion and internal competition for power can rapidly degenerate into conflict.

Identifying appropriate projects

One good way of gaining credibility and authority is to successfully work through a number of stages. These may be decided by the generation currently in charge, or by an agreement between the two generations. Working and studying outside the company can be the first steps. Then, when the next generation moves inside the firm, it can progress from managing a project, to a team, and then a division.

Each project must be chosen with care: it must involve a realistic objective and present a genuine challenge. At each stage, the level of competence attained must be assessed and performance evaluated. This will allow young employees to increase their standing, improve, and progress within the firm.

If succession involves a number of members of the next generation working in the company (siblings, cousins, etc.), care should be taken to include projects which will enable them to work together. This will also be a good way of pinpointing and defusing internal rivalries and power struggles within the family. Molding a well-integrated, efficient family team takes time and patience.

Performance assessment

As well as laying down the criteria to be used in the assessment, it is crucial to decide who will actually make that assessment. One way of ensuring objectivity is to set up a team comprising members from both inside and outside the company: a vice-president, someone from human resources, a member of the family, a consultant, a representative of the board of directors, and so on. Those selected must be trustworthy and experienced, and must have the best interests of the business and the family at heart. They should assess performance and offer feedback which, whether positive or negative, is objective and constructive.

The team will also be responsible for maintaining the correct balance between the professional aptitudes of the successors (technical skills, leadership, entrepreneurial spirit, vision, etc.) and their personal skills (family culture, values, family spirit, desire for continuity, etc.). It takes more than simply having the right name, being a good manager, or mastering the trade of the company to successfully lead a family business.

Women in the family business

A survey has shown that in 34% of family businesses in the U.S. the next CEO will be a woman, and that where the position will be filled by two or more people, almost half will have a woman as part of the team.[1] This rising trend can also be seen at work in Europe, albeit far more slowly and cautiously, and may well soon be mirrored in other cultures. It is mainly due to the fact that, today, women pursue the same educational paths as men. They take part in team sports just as much as men do, and this enables them to develop their competitive spirit. Since often they are not yet automatically groomed to take over a business, they tend to be more combative in order to prove what they can do.

Women have much to contribute to the company, and there is of course every reason to accord them a full role in the succession. They are generally more participatory and foster team spirit, while men are often more centered on themselves and concerned with acquiring power. Women will tend to seek harmony and endeavor to resolve conflicts.

---

1. Mass Mutual Financial Group survey, Raymond Institute, USA, 2003

The golden rules

Tact and diplomacy: To successfully enter and feel at home in a company, young people must understand that they cannot change everything overnight, and that the company has a past (presumably a successful one) which deserves respect. Changes will certainly have to be made; but in most cases they should be made gradually and subtly. Working in a family business often requires considerably more tact than working in any other kind of company.

Career plan: In order to avoid illusions and frustrations, and to prevent the succession process from becoming bogged down, it is important to draw up a career plan within the company, setting out the various stages and the length of time allocated for each stage.

Mentor: A mentor who guides, supports and advises a young person could well be their most valuable asset. Whether male or female, from within the company or outside, the mentor must be chosen by the next generation. Mentors must also be competent, fair and objective, and have a good understanding of family businesses.

VIII
The shareholders

Unlike conventional shareholders, who generally hold only a very small proportion of shares in a company, the shareholders in a family business possess a large part of the shares and voting rights. This gives them considerable influence over corporate affairs and strategic decisions affecting the business.

The power of shareholders

In fact, if they hold a controlling interest or the majority of the voting rights, theirs is the greatest power in the company. Few people, however, whether inside or outside the business, are aware of this fact, including many family shareholders themselves.

At the same time, this kind of power also necessitates intensive and targeted training for successors, whether or not they work in the business. While different from that of management, the training given to family shareholders must be specialized and of high quality. It must enable them to add real value to the business by making informed decisions.

Exploring different roles

No company is made up of its CEO alone, nor is it built solely on its various managers. It is easy to assume that those who do not want to work in the business can be of no use to it, and that there is no point worrying about them. But this is not true. The more successful such people are in their own chosen careers, the stronger and more fulfilled they will be in general, and the better they can be at the job of being a shareholder in the family business.

Shareholders who are asked to sit on the board of directors will be expected to have comprehensive training and an in-depth knowledge of the business. But shareholders can also explore a variety of other roles—as ambassadors, or as part of a special governing structure, such as a family council directing internal matters, a shareholders' committee overseeing property issues, or a foundation. Such a profusion of structures will increase the need for energy and leadership. Functions like these can also provide excellent springboards for young people, who learn how to work in a team and assess their own creativity and flexibility, as well as how to preserve family harmony.

A case study: maximizing shareholder effect

The shareholders in one major industrial family-owned group are forbidden to work in the company. This state of affairs may be unthinkable to many, but the family has a perfectly sound reason for enforcing it. Here the key question is, how can the family add value to its business?

First of all, this family is ecologically aware, applying the most stringent environmental protection laws both to itself and to the business. Additionally, the shareholders act as roving representatives of the company. They visit the group's factories, take an interest in its employees and production processes, ask questions, and are therefore able to measure directly the effect they have on the staff. All the same, they do not make decisions; that is management's responsibility.

Although its members pursue a wide range of professional interests, the family is thus very involved with the business and its activities. The shareholders make a significant contribution to its success, and are proud of their role.

IX

Challenges

These days, despite all the progress made in the field of family business, far too many successions still take place without proper planning and preparation for the next generation. The handover can come like a bolt from the blue following an accident or a death, and thus jeopardizes both the business and the relations within the family. It often pitches the next generation headlong into its new responsibilities, and abruptly curtails the time set aside for training or earning one's stripes "on the outside."

Watchwords: patience, trust, and transparency

It is essential that the succession process begin long before the actual handover—in a family business, successions cannot take place overnight, and patience is required from all concerned. Mutual trust is crucial. Succession must be seen as a challenge to be met together, as a team and with transparency throughout. Above all, triumphs great and small must be celebrated so that no one loses sight of what has already been achieved.

Building professional and family relationships

It should not be forgotten that working within a family business need not be a chore. In fact, many young people actively want to work with their mothers and fathers, especially when the latter are successful. Two generations working side by side as equals can do the company a world of good by combining energy with wisdom.

All the same, working well together means that certain rules and limits need to be respected and the right balance found between the distance typical of the relationship between employee and employer, and the intimacy of the connection between parent and child.

Most important of all is to let the family continue to be a family, and not become simply an extension of the business. The family must be able to enjoy something other than shoptalk; young people need a family environment in which they can share their sorrows, worries, joy and laughter. It is this sharing that helps maintain family unity within the business.

Making the choice

Sooner or later, young people have to decide whether or not to join the business. Of course, like any choice, this automatically means giving up the option not chosen. Joining the family business entails giving up the possibility of a career elsewhere, while not joining means giving up a part of one's own history. Whatever choice is made, the main thing is to be truly motivated by and for the path chosen. If that path is a career outside the business, this means being a fulfilled and contented shareholder ready to contribute much of his or her time. Choosing to join the firm, meanwhile, requires identification with the business and a passion for its products that will serve as a powerful driver of company performance.

Shedding the burden of the past

Many young people are afraid that they will not measure up to previous generations, so it is a good idea to "demystify" those generations and put the image of the all-powerful father into perspective. Memories of the past tend to focus only on the highlights; in fact, the success of a company is the positive overall outcome of a series of triumphs and failures. Previous generations have also made their share of mistakes.

Preserving family values

Successful families are often quite modest. They know that success is built on patience and no one is entirely safe from a fall. Members of such families work hard; they respect one another and their staff. These are personal qualities which in general will also permeate the corporate culture of their businesses.

When the family grows, the challenge is to preserve the same values for all its branches. A common phenomenon is the development of two opposing groups, the hard workers and the "spoiled brats". How can such groups be reconciled and conflict avoided? Some families go so far as to hire outsiders to do the work of CEO or director, and provide a buffer between these two warring factions.

Stating principles and values is one thing, but respecting commitments is another. When members of the senior generation retire, they must indicate their clear desire to do so by giving the date of their departure and keeping to their plan. Actions speak louder than words in such cases. In order to remain credible, they must ensure that what they communicate is consistent with what they actually do.

Taking risks and making innovations

Young people are often told by their elders to make their mark and distinguish themselves from the previous generation. But this can raise questions of its own: "What does that mean? Can we really do things our own way?"

After all, it is not exactly easy to be an innovator within a family business. Besides, is one even given the opportunity to do anything new? Naturally, it all depends on the circumstances. Some companies' need for innovation—in products, technology, work processes, organization, etc—is less urgent than that of others. Where the need is not immediate, the major task may be to preserve rather than innovate. Whatever the case, the next generation will need to know how to adapt, to take risks, and to be different. As for the senior generation, it should take on the role of encouraging its successors' taste for risk and innovation while ensuring that this is done with proper risk management.

Delegating real responsibility

Young people are under a great deal of pressure in the company: "We must not fail; too many people are just waiting for it to happen." The best way to deal with this is to be responsible and have a healthy dose of self-confidence. Parents can help build that confidence by assigning real responsibilities.

Parents do their children no service at all by being over-protective and shielding them from failure. By confronting them with their responsibilities from an early age and giving them candid feedback on their actual abilities, they can help their children develop fully and acquire a high degree of professional self-assurance. Equally, though, when giving their children responsibilities, parents must also be prepared to let them fail, and must support them in times of doubt.

Succession is like an obstacle course. But there is still a motivation for a young person to join the family business, and it can be summed up in the following statement: "Taking on the challenge brings with it both an obligation and a sense of pride, as well as a responsibility. If I didn't at least try it, I think I would regret it for the rest of my life."

Conclusion

For all their challenges, family businesses offer some significant advantages. They provide stability and long-term performance, and thus secure both jobs and stable profits. Above all, however, by concentrating capital and voting rights, they offer unparalleled managerial freedom. Controlling voting rights means the ability to make swift decisions and access to virtually unrestricted investment choices. If well managed, a family business can be a formidable asset for both the family as a whole and for the next generation in particular.

We want to close with a special message for that next generation: you are our future and our continuity. Be yourselves, enjoy what you do, and we are willing to bet that, despite all the hurdles that lie ahead, you will surprise and astonish us.

"There are two lasting bequests we can give our children.
One is roots. The other is wings."
Hodding Carter, J.R.

BIBLIOGRAPHY

Aronoff, C.E., J. H. Astrachan, and J.L. Ward, *Developing Family Business Policies: Your Guide to the Future.* Marietta, Georgia, Family Enterprise Publishers, 1998.

Aronoff, C.E., J.H. Astrachan, and J.L. Ward, *Family Business Sourcebook 3rd edition.* Marietta, Georgia, Family Enterprise Publishers, 2002.

Aronoff, C.E., S. L. McClure, and J.L. Ward, *Family Business Succession: The Final Test of Greatness.* Marietta, Georgia, Family Enterprise Publishers, 2003.

Astrachan, J.H., and K. Macmillan, *Conflict & Communication,* Marietta, Georgia, Family Enterprise Publishers, 2003.

Astrachan, J.H., et al., Mass Mutual Survey, USA, 2003.

Carlock, R.S., and J.L. Ward, *Strategic Planning for the Family Business,* New York, Palgrave Macmillan, 2001.

Gersick, K.E., J.A. Davis, M. McCollom Hampton, and I. Lansberg, *Generation to Generation: Life Cycles of the Family Business,* Boston, Harvard Business School Press, 1997.

Kenyon-Rouvinez, D., G. Adler, G. Corbetta, and G. Cuneo, *Sharing Wisdom, Building Values. Letters From Family Business Owners To Their Successors*. Marietta, Georgia, Family Enterprise Publishers, 2002.

Kenyon-Rouvinez, D., Ward, J.L., *Family Business: Key Issues,* London, Palgrave Macmillan, 2004.

Lansberg, I., *Succeeding Generations: Realizing the Dream of Families in Business,* Boston, Harvard Business School Press, 1999.

Schwass, J., *Wise Growth Strategies in Leading Family Businesses,* London, Palgrave Macmillan, 2005.

Van der Heyden, L., C. Blondel, and R. S. Carlock, Fair Process: Striving for Justice in Family Business, *Family Business Review,* Vol. 18, March 2005, Kennesaw, Georgia, pp. 1-21.

Ward, J.L., *Perpetuating the Family Business,* London, Palgrave Macmillan, 2004.

Detailed table of contents

Foreword, Thierry Lombard 7
Introduction 13
Chapitre 1. Succession 15
    A joint venture between two generations 18
    Sharing out 20
    A fair process 22
    The family constitution 24
    The role of the parents 26
    The role of the children 28
    A success story 30
Chapitre 2. Communication 33
    Communication within the family 34
    Communication within the business 36
    Communication outside the business 36
    Expectations 38
    Conflict 40
    Managing conflicts 42
Chapitre 3. The family 47
    The definition of "family" 50
    The tools available to families 52
    Family spirit 52
    A code of conduct 54
    Family meetings 54
    The family council 54
Chapitre 4. The name 57
    The impact of the name on the next generation 58
    Striking the right balance 60
    A powerful management tool 62

Chapitre 5. Identity 65
   The need to exist. 68
   The fundamental questions 70

Chapitre 6. Preparing to join the business 73
   Studies and training 76
   The benefits of training. 78
   The role of the family 80
   Should I or shouldn't I?. 82

Chapitre 7. Working in the company 87
   Relationships with employees 90
   Identifying appropriate projects. 92
   Performance assessment. 94
   Women in the family business. 96
   The golden rules. 98

Chapitre 8. The shareholders 101
   The power of shareholders 102
   Exploring different roles 104
   A case study: maximizing shareholder effect 106

Chapitre 9. Challenges 109
   Watchwords: patience, trust, and transparency 110
   Building professional and family relationships 112
   Making the choice 114
   Shedding the burden of the past. 114
   Preserving family values 116
   Taking risks and making innovations. 118
   Delegating real responsibility 120

Conclusion 123
Bibliography 125
Index 128

INDEX

Absence of interest, 84
Ambitions, 80
Anecdotes, 60
Arrogance, 58
Attention, 42
Autority, 93
Career plan, 98
Challenges, 109
Child's upbringing, 16
Code of conduct, 54
Communication outside the business, 36
Communication within the business, 36
Communication within the family, 36
Communication, 33
Connexion with the product, 84
Consumers, 62
Corporate culture, 52
Credibility, 90
Customers, 36
Decision-making power, 16
Definition of "family", 50
Dual identity, 60
Dual, 98
Employers, 36
Energy, 42
Eponymous companies, 58
Equality, 22
Expectations, 38
Family constitution, 24
Family council, 54
Family events, 44
Family meetings, 54
Family values, 28, 116

Feed-back, 94
Feeling of injustice, 50
Feelings, 48
Frustrations, 50
Generations, 18
Harmony, 44
History, 52
Identification, 114
Identifying appropriate projects, 92
Identity, 65
Image, 58
In-laws, 50
Innovation, 118
Level of competence, 92
Limitation, 58
Loneliness, 68
Love, 34
Management tool, 62
Managing conflicts, 42
Mentor, 98
Motivation, 28
Need to exist, 68
Non motivation, 28
Open mind, 44
Ownership succession, 16
Passion, 88
Patience, 110
Performance assessment, 94
Personal skills, 94
Position, 38
Preparation, 73
Presence of the family, 62
Pride, 60

Product, 60
Professional aptitudes, 94
Profitability, 48
Quality, 62
Relationship, 48
Relationships with employees, 90
Reputation, 60
Responsabilities, 120
Right balance, 60
Right to make mistakes, 82
Role of the family, 80
Role of the parents, 26
Rumors, 36
Security, 62
Self-confidence, 120
Sens of duty, 60
Shame, 84
Share, 20
Shareholders power, 102
Shareholders, 101
Sharing of family values, 16
Socialization, 74
Studies, 76
Succession, 15
Sucess, 30
Tact, 98
Taste of worklife, 74
The name, 57
Training, 28, 76
Transparency, 110
Trust, 110
Voting rights, 16